William Sh
King Lear

Written by William Shakespeare
Adapted by Timothy Knapman
Illustrated by Ollie Cuthbertson

For Michael and Edward, with love TK

Published by Pearson Education Limited, Edinburgh Gate, Harlow, Essex, CM20 2JE.
www.pearsonschools.co.uk

Text © Timothy Knapman 2013
Designed by Vincent Shaw-Morton
Original illustrations © Pearson Education Limited 2013
Illustrated by Ollie Cuthbertson, The Bright Agency

The right of Timothy Knapman to be identified as author of this work has been asserted by him in accordance with the Copyright, Designs and Patents Act 1988.

First published 2013

17 16 15 14 13
10 9 8 7 6 5 4 3 2 1

British Library Cataloguing in Publication Data
A catalogue record for this book is available from the British Library

ISBN 978 0 435 14444 9

Copyright notice
All rights reserved. No part of this publication may be reproduced in any form or by any means (including photocopying or storing it in any medium by electronic means and whether or not transiently or incidentally to some other use of this publication) without the written permission of the copyright owner, except in accordance with the provisions of the Copyright, Designs and Patents Act 1988 or under the terms of a licence issued by the Copyright Licensing Agency, Saffron House, 6–10 Kirby Street, London EC1N 8TS (www.cla.co.uk). Applications for the copyright owner's written permission should be addressed to the publisher.

Printed and bound in Dubai by Oriental Press.

Acknowledgements
We would like to thank Bangor Central Integrated Primary School, Northern Ireland; Bishop Henderson Church of England Primary School, Somerset; Bletchingdon Parochial Church of England Primary School, Oxfordshire; Brookside Community Primary School, Somerset; Bude Park Primary School, Hull; Carisbrooke Church of England Primary School, Isle of Wight; Cheddington Combined School, Buckinghamshire; Dair House Independent School, Buckinghamshire; Glebe Infant School, Gloucestershire; Henley Green Primary School, Coventry; Lovelace Primary School, Surrey; Our Lady of Peace Junior School, Slough; Tackley Church of England Primary School, Oxfordshire; and Twyford Church of England School, Buckinghamshire for their invaluable help in the development and trialling of the Bug Club resources.

Every effort has been made to contact copyright holders of material reproduced in this book. Any omissions will be rectified in subsequent printings if notice is given to the publishers.

Contents

Chapter 1
A Kingdom Divided — 6

Chapter 2
A Brother Betrayed — 18

Chapter 3
Punishment — 32

Chapter 4
Into the Storm — 42

Chapter 5
The Lowest of the Low — 53

Chapter 6
Blinded — 63

Chapter 7
Enemies — 72

Chapter 8
The Great Fall — 83

Chapter 9
War — 95

Chapter 10
All for Nothing — 107

MAIN CHARACTERS

King Lear

Goneril	Regan	Cordelia
+	+	+
Duke of Albany	Duke of Cornwall	(marries King of France)

OTHER CHARACTERS

Earl of Kent – King Lear's most loyal subject and friend

The Fool – the king's jester, a wise figure who highlights King Lear's foolish behaviour

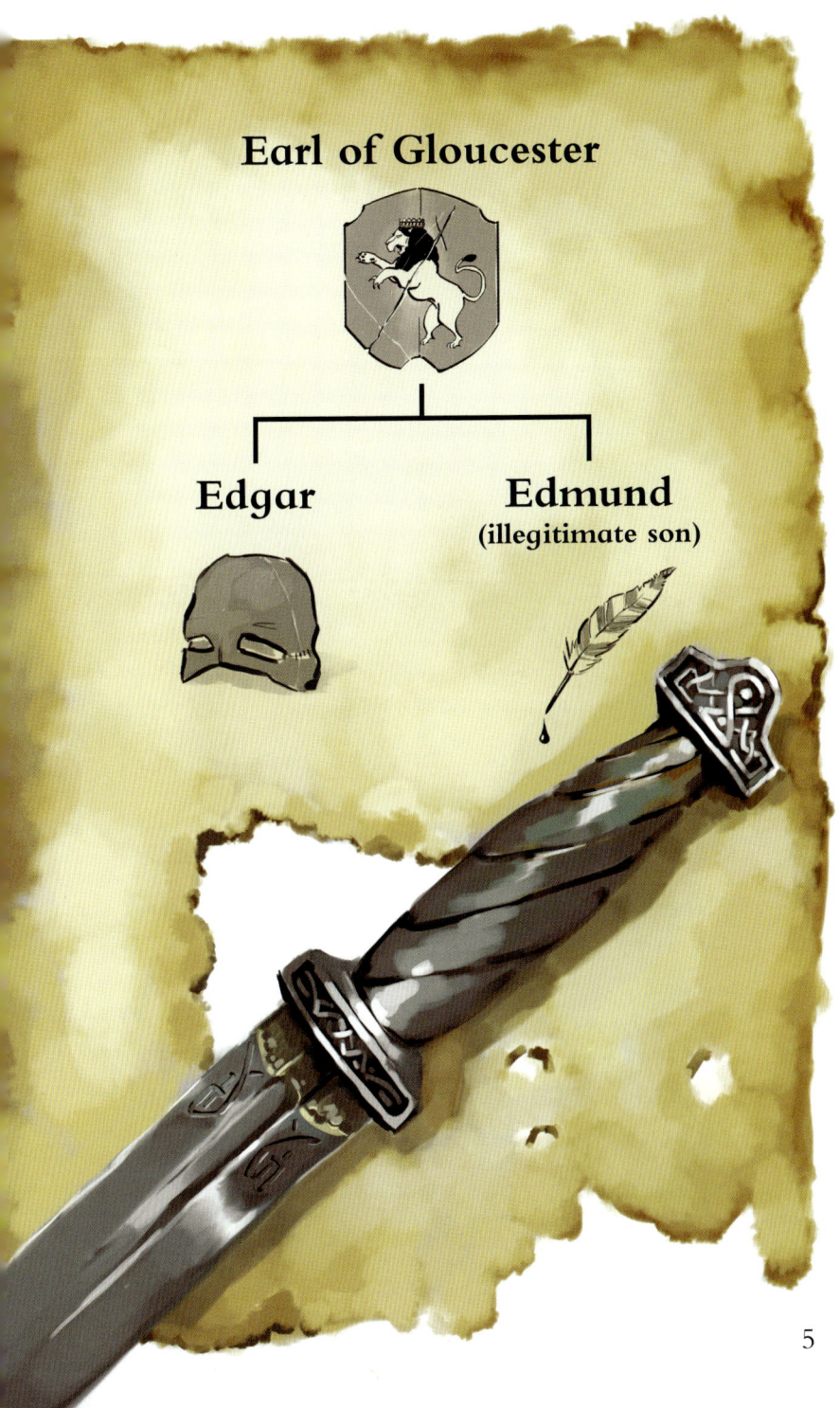

CHAPTER ONE
A Kingdom Divided

It couldn't be true.

The rumour had started at first light and ran through the castle like wildfire. Everyone had heard it, from the sentries standing guard at the top of the tallest towers to the miserable prisoners down in the deepest dungeons.

Few could believe it. Those who did thought that old King Lear had gone mad at last.

But everyone agreed: if it *were* true, then no good could come of it.

Suddenly the trumpets blared to summon all the lords and ladies to the throne room and there was no point gossiping any more. They would soon find out the truth.

"That is Princess Goneril, the king's eldest daughter, and that's her husband, the Duke of Albany," the Earl of Gloucester whispered to his son, Edmund, as they watched the royal family take their places in the throne room. "And over there is Princess Regan and *her* husband, the Duke of Cornwall."

All his life, Edmund had secretly dreamed of being rich and powerful, but this was the first time he'd been to court – the first time he'd been this close to the really important people in the land.

"And who is *that*? sighed Edmund"

"Princess Cordelia, the king's youngest and favourite daughter," replied Gloucester.

"She's beautiful!" said Edmund.

"And destined to marry either the Duke of Burgundy or the King of France," Gloucester chuckled to his son, "so don't go getting any ideas!"

Edmund chuckled along with his father, but inwardly he was furious: no one was too good for him to marry – not even a princess!

"Gloucester, my old friend!" said a voice behind them, and they turned around. The speaker was powerfully built, with a great beard, and he grabbed Gloucester in a friendly bear-hug.

"And this is the Earl of Kent," said Gloucester. "A great soldier, and the king's most loyal subject!"

Before Kent could say anything, another fanfare sounded. The king was coming.

At once, everyone sank to their knees, but even with his head bowed Edmund managed to steal a look at King Lear as he came in. He was beautifully dressed, and must have been a powerful warrior once, but he was old now – eighty at least, Edmund supposed.

He could hear the king sigh as he sank down onto his throne.

The lords and ladies got to their feet.

"Gloucester," said King Lear – his voice was still strong and commanding – "ask our guests, the King of France and the Duke of Burgundy, to join us now. It is time they found out which one of them is to marry Princess Cordelia."

"Yes, sire," said Gloucester with a bow, and he hastened from the room.

"The rest of you, I have an announcement to make," said the king. "Fetch the map!"

He waved his hand and four servants immediately brought in a huge map of the kingdom of Britain.

"I am old," said the king, "and I want to enjoy what little life I have left. So I have decided that, from now on, I shall spend my days hunting and feasting with my knights. You'll still call me 'king' and treat me just the same as you always did – but my daughters are to rule in my place."

People gasped. So the rumour was true!

"I will divide this kingdom into three," said the king, "and each of them will have her share."

Turning to his daughters, he said, "Ah, but which of you gets the best bit, my darlings? That's easy. It will be the one of you who loves me most."

The king looked like someone who had invented a new party game and couldn't wait to start playing it.

"Tell me, Goneril," he went on, "how much do you love me?"

The king's eldest daughter replied immediately.

"I love you more than I can possibly say," she said. "More than eyesight, as much as life. More than any child ever loved a father."

The king smiled and nodded.

"Then this share of the kingdom, with all its rich farmland and mighty forests is yours," he said, and he drew his sword and cut the shape of Goneril's lands out of the map. Then he turned to his middle daughter. "What do you say, Regan?"

"I agree with everything my sister said," replied Regan, "except that I don't think she went far enough. I love nothing and no one but you."

Again, the king looked pleased.

"Then you must have this share, which is just as good as Goneril's," he said, and cut Regan as large a slice of the map. "And now, my youngest and my joy: Cordelia. What can you say to earn a share of this kingdom that is richer by far than the ones I just gave your sisters?"

Cordelia didn't answer at once. She thought for a long time and eventually she said, "Nothing."

The king laughed. He thought she was just joking.

"You'll get nothing for 'nothing'," he said. "Say more."

But Cordelia wasn't joking.

"I cannot," she said. "I love you; of course I do. You're my father – but when I marry, I will love my husband just as much – more even. That's only right. Why did my sisters get married, if they were just going to love you and no one else?"

The king looked heartbroken.

"Do you mean what you say?" he asked. He sounded like a little boy who hadn't got what he wanted for Christmas.

"I could never lie to you," said Cordelia steadily, as she looked into her father's eyes.

"Very well then!" roared the king – who was suddenly and frighteningly furious. "If 'nothing' is what you say, nothing is what you'll get! No lands, no love – nothing! You are no longer my daughter!"

"Sire, please, no!" cried Kent, rushing forward. "Can't you see that she's telling the truth? It's the other two who are lying so they can get what they want. They don't love you; they only love what they can take from you!"

"Silence, Kent!" the king shrieked. "I loved her most, and I'd hoped that she'd look after me now I'm old. Instead of that, she has broken my heart! Regan and Goneril, divide the kingdom between you. I don't care how!"

With that, he took the crown from his head and threw it at them.

Regan and Goneril leapt for it like bridesmaids at a wedding, jumping for the bouquet.

"You old fool! You're making a terrible mistake!" cried Kent – and, again, gasps filled the throne room. Kent stopped – and took a breath. "Forgive me, sire. I beg you – as your most loyal, true and humble servant – please think again before it's too late!"

"How dare you speak to your king like that?" shouted Lear. "Kent, you are banished! Get out of my sight – and if you ever dare return to Britain, I will have you executed."

"Very well," said Kent. "But you will regret this!" He strode out of the throne room. As he passed Cordelia, he said, "The gods protect you, Princess."

Kent walked straight into Gloucester in the corridor outside.

"What's happened?" Gloucester asked.

"You'll find out soon enough," said Kent.

"Watch yourself, my friend. These are difficult times."

Then he was gone.

Bewildered, Gloucester led the King, of France and the Duke of Burgundy into the throne room. The moment he saw him, Gloucester knew that King Lear had just thrown one of his tantrums.

"Honoured guests," growled King Lear. "I am sorry to say that I can no longer offer a dowry for my … for this young woman." He pointed at Cordelia and Gloucester saw that she had been crying. "Which of you can take her off my hands for…" he spat the word out, "*'nothing'*?"

"Sire, Burgundy is proud, but we are poor," said the duke. "I can't afford to marry her if you don't pay me her dowry. I am sorry."

The King of France stepped forward. "Cordelia," he said, "I have loved you from the first moment I saw you. I don't care if you have no money – for if you truly love me, that is more riches than I have ever dreamed of having! Will you marry me?"

Despite her distress, Cordelia couldn't stop herself smiling.

"Of course I will," she said.

"Take her then," sneered Lear, and he rose and hobbled off out of the throne room.

As she passed Goneril and Regan, Cordelia said, "Look after our father. I still love him, and I only hope you meant at least some of what you said to him."

"The days when you told us what to do are over, little sister!" Regan spat back at her.

"Oh, my poor father," said Cordelia.

"He has made his choice," said the King of France, "and I have made mine. Come. My ship is waiting to take us home."

By now people were streaming out of the throne room, muttering uneasily.

Edmund lingered, watching as Goneril and Regan whispered to each other. *What are they plotting?* he wondered.

In a matter of minutes, King Lear had turned the world upside down.

The mighty had fallen and there was a new power in the land. Now anything at all could happen.

Edmund had an idea.

CHAPTER TWO
A Brother Betrayed

Edmund did a lot of thinking on the journey back to his father's castle. He had always known that he deserved to become the next Earl of Gloucester when his father died. He was brave and clever and, more importantly, he didn't let things like kindness or mercy cloud his thinking. If something had to be done, he would do it, and never mind who had to suffer.

The problem was that the law wouldn't allow it.

The law said that a man's first-born son had to inherit everything, and Edmund had an older brother called Edgar. Foolish, trusting, lazy-brained Edgar! He even had a big fat 'G' for 'good' planted right in the middle of his name in case you ever forgot how wonderful he was! Edmund thought about the 'M' that crouched like a venomous spider in the middle of *his* name: 'M' for 'monster' – and for 'missing out'.

For the rest of his life, Edmund would be second best: pushed into the shadows and given nothing except out of the kindness of his brother's heart. What had Edgar done to deserve his good fortune? He'd got himself born twelve months before Edmund, that was all. It made Edmund's blood boil!

Edgar was a healthy young man. There was no chance that disease would carry him off to an early grave and allow Edmund to inherit and so, for years, Edmund had despaired of ever getting what he deserved.

Until the day the king changed everything.

Before Edmund's eyes, the king had shown the world that it didn't matter when you were born. He had divided his kingdom – while he was still alive, mind you! – and made his daughters compete for it!

If there was one thing Edmund was good at, it was a competition – especially if you earned extra points for being devious.

By the time his horse galloped across the drawbridge, Edmund knew what to do. Within ten minutes of reaching his room in the East Tower, he had done it.

His brother's handwriting was very easy to forge.

"My dear brother Edmund," Edmund wrote. "How much longer do we have to be told what to do by a stupid old man? Our father must be so bored with still being alive – just as I am bored with waiting for him to die. When I am earl, it will all be different, and if you help me get him out of the way, I promise to give you half my fortune. Your loving brother and soon to be (if you're with me) Earl of Gloucester. Edgar."

The ink was scarcely dry when Edmund heard his father's slow footsteps on the stairs outside. Just as the old man walked in,

Edmund made a move to hide the letter – making sure that his father noticed exactly what he was doing.

"What's that you've got there?" asked Gloucester, puzzled.

"It's nothing, Father," said Edmund innocently.

"It's not nothing, is it? It's a letter. Show me," said Gloucester.

"It's just a bit of nonsense, I'm sure," said Edmund. "A joke."

"Show it to me," said Gloucester – his voice now slow and deep: the voice of a man who did not want to be argued with.

"Very well," said Edmund, and he handed the letter over.

Edmund took great care not to smile as he watched his father's face become angrier and angrier.

"What is the meaning of this?" the old man roared. "Where is your brother?"

"Father, wait!" Edmund stopped his father storming out of his room. "We don't know

"Not written by him?" said Gloucester. "It's signed by him, isn't it? It's his handwriting!"

"I know this looks bad," said Edmund. "Let me talk to him. I'm sure there's been some kind of misunderstanding."

Gloucester looked deep into Edmund's eyes. It was obvious he trusted him, the silly old fool!

"Edgar doesn't deserve a brother so loyal," said Gloucester. "But if you find out that he *did* write this, you come straight to me and tell me. You promise?"

"Of course, Father," said Edmund.

Gloucester's shoulders fell. For the second time in as many days, Edmund saw the heartbreak of an old man disappointed by his favourite child.

Edgar was where he always was: in the library, reading.

"There you are, brother!" Edmund gasped. He'd run all the way there. It was important for his plan that he should find Edgar before their father did.

"Edmund, how lovely to see you! How was court?" said Edgar, smiling and friendly as always.

"Never mind that now!" said Edmund. "You're in great danger."

"I'm sorry?" Edgar laughed. His life had been so lucky, so protected, that he clearly couldn't imagine that anything bad would ever happen to him.

"Father's gone mad," Edmund whispered. "I don't know why. He is very angry with you. What did you say to him?"

"Nothing," said Edgar, his smile fading.

"Are you sure?" said Edmund. "He said he wants you dead."

"*Dead?*" said Edgar, and Edmund enjoyed the look of fear on his face.

"I'll speak to him," Edmund went on. "I'll see if I can get him to calm down. In the meantime, I suggest you find somewhere to hide – and if you do go out, make sure you take your sword."

Edgar embraced Edmund.

"I don't deserve a brother so loyal," he said as they parted.

And I don't deserve brother so stupid, but I've got one, thought Edmund as he watched him slip out of the library.

Edmund smiled. It was all going better than he could have hoped.

Kent looked at his reflection in the stream. He'd shaved off his beard and, in the shabby clothes of a peasant, he was unrecognisable.

He was good at disguising his voice, too. No one would ever know it was him.

Of course, he should have just done what the king ordered: left the country to make a new life for himself abroad. The problem was that Kent loved his king – no matter how stupid and stubborn he could be. He knew that old Lear had made a terrible mistake, and he couldn't bear to think of him left to the mercy of those two scheming daughters of his, Goneril and Regan.

Kent was a man of honour. He had sworn to protect King Lear to his dying day and that was why he was here, waiting outside Goneril's castle for Lear and his hundred knights to return from another day's hunting.

At last they did, drunkenly singing and laughing. Kent went up to Lear and bowed his head.

"Begging your pardon, sir," said Kent, "but I'm an honest fellow, strong and loyal, and I am in need of a master to serve."

"Well I'm in need of my dinner," said Lear. "Where is my daughter? She should be here to welcome us back from the hunt."

The only person who emerged from Goneril's castle was a puffed-up servant in a silly hat.

"My lady is too busy to greet you this evening," said the servant. He looked like there was a nasty smell just under his nose.

"Too busy?" roared Lear. "You do know who I am, you strutting popinjay?"

"You are my lady's father," said the servant.

Kent knew that was going too far. Lear no longer ruled the country, it was true, but he still deserved to be treated with all the honour due to a king.

"Hey you! Show some respect!" Kent snapped and he knocked the servant's silly hat off his head and into a patch of mud. Lear and his knights roared with laughter.

"How dare you touch me!" cried the servant, bending down to pick his hat up.

"I'll do more than touch you, if you talk to this gentleman like that again!" Kent said, and he kicked the servant so hard he landed face down in the mud.

"Strong and loyal, you say?" said Lear, laughing. "There will always be a place for you at my side."

Lear's Fool was waiting for them in the great hall of the castle. He was dressed in his jester's cap and bells but, instead of greeting the hunting party with a joke or a song, he stared miserably at them.

"Why are you looking so gloomy, Fool?" asked Lear.

"Why shouldn't I?" said the Fool. "I handed over everything I had to people who hate me. Oh no, wait a minute – that was you. I think one of us is in the wrong job."

"Are you calling me a fool?" said Lear.

"You gave away your title," said the Fool, "– that one you were born with."

"What do you mean by that?" said Lear, reaching for his whip.

"Nothing," said the Fool. "And you can't punish me for that. *'You'll get nothing for "nothing"'* don't forget."

The Fool was the only one of Lear's servants who was allowed to talk to him like that: it was part of his job — to tell Lear the truth when no one else dared to. Still, there were times when Lear didn't want to hear the truth.

He was relieved to see the great doors of the hall swing open and his daughter Goneril walk in with her mud-spattered servant at her side.

"At last!" said Lear. "My daughter is kind enough to see me! But what's she got to frown about?"

"I remember the days when *she* was worried when *you* frowned," said the Fool. "But that was before you made your daughters into your parents. You should watch out — it looks as if you're going to get a right telling-off. She might even give you a spanking!"

"My dear father," said Goneril, "I am very sorry, but I cannot let this go on any longer. The behaviour of your – *friends* ..."– she said the word with great distaste – "is ruining my life and my home. They are drunken and noisy – they fight, they break things, they make a mess everywhere – and now they have humiliated poor Oswald here, my most loyal servant. Look at him – he's absolutely covered in mud."

Oswald looked spitefully at Kent.

"It is too much!" said Goneril. "It's high time you got rid of them and spent your remaining days with quieter, wiser, sober men, as befits a man of your age."

"'A man of my age'?" roared Lear. "How dare you? Who are you to tell me what I can and can't do? I tell you who you're *not* – you're no daughter of mine! Well, you needn't worry yourself any more, madam! Not for one moment am I going to stay where I'm not wanted!"

"That's not what I said," Goneril sighed, tired of her father's tantrums.

"Pack up, everyone!" said Lear. "I still have Regan – one daughter I can trust! We'll go and stay with her."

"Father!" Goneril shouted after him.

"Not another word!" cried Lear. "You ungrateful harpy! I curse you! Oh gods, if you can hear me, I beg you: shrivel up her insides and make sure that this … *creature* here never gives birth! She knows nothing of the loyalty, of the trust – of the *love* that should bind a parent to a child! You know who would never have done this to me? My darling Cordel …"

Lear stopped. He was shaking. He ran his hand over his cheek. It was wet with tears.

"Fool," he said, "what is happening to me? Am I going mad?"

"Either that," said the Fool, "or at long last you're coming to your senses."

CHAPTER THREE
Punishment

Gloucester's castle was crawling with guards — all of them under orders to find his son, Edgar. The search had become more urgent when Lear's middle daughter, Regan, sent word that she and her husband, the Duke of Cornwall, were to visit that day. Gloucester wanted the matter settled before they arrived: he couldn't bear the shame of having to explain to them that his beloved son had become a murderous traitor.

Edmund ducked round a corner as a patrol passed. He had taken great care that he wasn't being followed as he made his way to the old stables. He didn't want to give away his brother's hiding place – not just yet.

When at last he could be sure that no one was watching, he crossed the courtyard and slipped through a little door.

At once, his brother Edgar bounded out of the shadows to embrace him.

"Have you had a chance to talk to Father?" Edgar asked – his once handsome young face now lined with worry. "To explain that this is all some dreadful misunderstanding?"

"I'm sorry," Edmund said solemnly. "He wouldn't hear of it, but it's worse than that: he's found out where you're hiding."

"What? How could he?" said Edgar.

"I don't know," said Edmund. "They're on their way to arrest you right now, but if Father knows you've escaped, he might begin to see reason. The important thing is that you have to get away. You can't clear your name if you're stuck in the dungeon."

Edmund drew his sword.

"What are you doing?" said Edgar.

"It's part of my plan," said Edmund.

"If Father's seen we've been fighting – "
But before he could finish his sentence, they heard the deafening clatter of a heavily-armed patrol.

Right on time, thought Edmund, but what he said was, "You're just going to have to trust me. Do you trust me?"

"Of course," said Edgar without a moment's thought.

Then you deserve everything you get, thought Edmund, and he slashed at his brother with his sword.

Edgar only just managed to step out of the way of the blade. Confused, shaking, he drew his sword and he and Edmund began to fight.

"Guards! Guards! I've found him!" Edmund shouted.

The door flew open and the patrol burst in. The soldiers stood staring at the two brothers for a moment, unsure of what to do.

"This is your chance!" Edmund hissed at Edgar. "*Run!*"

Edgar pushed his way past the soldiers and ran off.

"Well what are you waiting for, you idiots?" Edmund roared at the nearby patrol. "After him!"

When they had gone, Edmund took a deep breath and cut himself on the arm with his own sword. *That should do the trick*, he thought, and he staggered out of the room and into the courtyard.

"Edmund? What's happened? What has he done to you?" It was Gloucester, his father. He must have heard the commotion and come running.

"I'm sorry, Father. I tried to stop him escaping, but when he realised I would never betray you, he drew his sword on me," said Edmund, trying hard to strike the right note of bravery mixed with disbelief.

"There can be no more room for doubt," said Gloucester, heavily. "He truly is a traitor, and I hereby sentence him to death. Have my soldiers proclaim it throughout my lands."

From the gates, trumpets sounded. Regan and Cornwall had arrived.

"Already?" groaned Gloucester. "Are my troubles never to end?"

When Lear heard that Regan had gone to Gloucester's castle, he sent Kent ahead with a message for her.

Kent hoped that Regan would look after her father better than Goneril had done, but, as he drew near the castle, he saw Oswald – Goneril's arrogant servant – on the road ahead of him. Goneril must have sent him with a message to Regan, trying to poison her mind against their father. Kent had to stop that message getting through.

"Hey, I know you!" he cried out. "You're that stuck-up servant!"

Oswald looked him up and down. "Well I'm sure I don't know you," he said pompously, and walked on towards the castle.

"Then let me give you a little reminder!" said Kent, and he pushed Oswald into the mud.

"Help!" Oswald shrieked. "I'm being attacked by a lunatic!"

"Oh! So I'm mad, am I?" said Kent. "Come here now!"

Oswald scrambled to his feet and Kent went after him, hoping that perhaps he could chase him away from the castle, but Oswald wouldn't stop shrieking and soon they'd caught the attention of the castle guards.

"What's going on here?"

Kent looked round. It was Edmund, the young man he'd met in Lear's throne room, and behind him his father, Gloucester, and Regan and Cornwall. Kent hoped that they wouldn't recognise him.

"This madman attacked me!" Oswald whined. "He's one of the king's servants. This is the second time he's pushed me!"

"So what if I did?" said Kent.

"Maybe you want to push my wife into the mud next, eh?" This was Cornwall – Regan's husband – who'd always fancied himself as a hard man. He walked up to Kent until his face was so close that Kent could smell the sour reek of meat on his breath. "Or the earl here? Or his son? Or me, perhaps?" There was an ugly relish in his eyes.

"Begging your pardon, sir," said Kent, "but I have a message from my master."

Cornwall snatched the letter out of his hand. Without reading it, he tore it up and said, "Put him in the stocks."

Gloucester gasped. Cornwall hadn't just shown gross disrespect to the king by tearing up his letter. The stocks were a harsh punishment: you were made to sit out in all weathers with your feet caught in a wooden frame, and passers-by could throw anything they wanted at you. If you were lucky, it was rotten fruit; if not, it was stones. People could die in the stocks. Kent saw Gloucester look across to Regan. There wasn't a flicker of mercy on Regan's face, so Gloucester nodded reluctantly to his guards and they carried out Cornwall's order.

Cornwall, Regan and Edmund watched till it was done and went back into the castle.

"I am sorry," said Gloucester, who still did not recognise his old friend. "I'll try and persuade them to let you go."

"Please don't bother, sir," said Kent, smiling bravely. "I needed some fresh air. Besides, my master will be along soon, and he will surely set me free."

Gloucester didn't look convinced, but he nodded and returned to the castle.

Edgar didn't stop running till he was many miles away. He heard his father's soldiers proclaiming the sentence of death and dire punishments for anyone who 'sheltered that most notorious traitor, the Earl of Gloucester's sometime son, Edgar'. It would not be enough for him just to keep moving. He needed a disguise – but what?

No one paid any attention to the Bedlam beggars – the poor mad souls who roamed the land, shunned and uncared for – he would pretend to be one of them. Poor Tom, that's what he'd call himself. If anyone looked too closely at him, he'd dribble and jabber and cry out – and he knew they would turn away in disgust.

Edmund tore his clothes and daubed himself in mud, and then a thought struck him: *What kind of a world was this, where the only thing that kept you safe was other people's heartlessness?*

CHAPTER FOUR
Into the Storm

Night fell and it grew bitterly cold. In the stocks outside Gloucester's castle, Kent was worried that he might actually freeze to death.

Overhead the clouds thickened and, from far away, he could hear thunder. A storm was brewing.

Kent tried to stay awake, knowing that if he did fall asleep he might never wake up again, but his eyelids were heavy as lead.

Then suddenly there were voices all around him, and the warm breath of horses pluming in torchlight. Lear had arrived at last!

"Your Majesty!" cried Kent.

"Who did this to you?" Lear roared.

"Cornwall", said Kent, "and Princess Regan."

"They knew you were my servant, and you carried a message from me?" said Lear.

"I did better than the message," said Kent. "Cornwall tore that to pieces."

"How dare he?" cried Lear, and he stormed off into the castle. "You wait till I get my hands on him!"

Kent's eyes grew accustomed to the flickering torchlight and he looked around him. There seemed to be fewer people with the king.

"What happened to the rest of his servants?" Kent asked the Fool.

"When a wheel starts to roll downhill," the Fool replied, "a wise man doesn't run after it. He might trip and break his neck."

So they've seen that Lear is losing his power and decided to desert him, Kent thought and he said, bitterly, "Where did you learn about what a wise man does, Fool?"

"Not in the stocks, that's for sure, Even Bigger Fool," was the reply.

Lear returned with Gloucester.

"What do you mean they're too tired to see me?" said Lear. "I am the king! If I want to speak to someone, they come running!"

"Of course, sire," said Gloucester, and he disappeared back inside the castle.

"Get him out of those damn things," Lear commanded, and Kent was set free.

Gloucester returned with Regan and Cornwall. Kent thought they didn't look happy to be roused from their beds and made to come out into the cold night. Still, they both bowed to Lear.

"At last!" Lear said. "Regan, you will not believe how Goneril has treated me! Ordering me about, telling me that I was making a mess of her castle, that I didn't need a hundred knights – I tell you, I wouldn't have believed such cruelty from a daughter was possible."

"I'm sure you must be mistaken, Father," said Regan.

"What?" said Lear. He sounded very surprised.

"My sister is a very kind and dutiful daughter," said Regan. "I know she had your best interests at heart. A man of your age needs looking after, and it's high time you realised that. My sister was only making sure you do what's best for you. Why don't you go back to her and apologise?"

"Apologise?" Lear roared. He was astounded. "To that bossy little witch? I'd rather die!"

Before he could go on, trumpets sounded. Kent looked round to see Goneril and her husband, Albany, arriving.

"So, this is where you've got to, Father," said Goneril. "We were worried sick about you!"

"Don't you call me 'Father', you festering sore!" said Lear. "A fat lot you care about me!"

"That's not fair!" said Regan. "It's as I said: my sister only wants what's best. Why don't you go back and stay with her until the end of the month? Then you can come and visit me."

"Oh yes, Father, do," said Goneril. "But he doesn't need all those knights, does he?" said Goneril.

"A hundred of them? Of course he doesn't," said Regan. "Surely he can make do with fifty."

"Twenty-five would be plenty," said Goneril.

"Ten would be quite enough," said Regan. "Or even five."

"Why does he need any at all?" said Goneril. "We have servants; if he wants something, all he has to do is ask one of them."

"That makes sense," said Regan.

All this time, Lear just stared at them.

"I cannot believe I am hearing this!" cried Lear. "I gave you everything!"

"And in your own good time you gave it," snapped Regan. Suddenly, her caring tone was gone and she was all anger.

"How could I have been so foolish?" said Lear. "I thought you loved me, but that was all lies, wasn't it? Well I'll be revenged on you, you greedy hags, oh yes! Just you wait until I … until I … I don't know what I'm going to do, but it will be horrible, I can promise you that!"

Kent couldn't bear to watch. The once great and powerful king had been reduced to name-calling and empty threats, like a silly little boy – and then the tears started again.

"No, I won't cry," said Lear. "I'd rather see the end of the world than show a single tear to you heartless monsters!" And then he lost control and began to bawl like a baby. "Oh, Fool, I *am* going mad!"

Lear gave a great cry and stumbled off into the darkness of the barren moorland that surrounded Gloucester's castle. Kent and the Fool went after him.

There was a deafening clap of thunder. The storm was about to break.

"We can't just let him go like that," said Gloucester. "He'll catch his death of cold."

"You heard what he said," replied Goneril. "Our father doesn't like being told what to do – *especially* if it's for his own good."

"I'm certainly not risking a soaking for his sake," said Regan. "Let's go back inside."

"Make sure the doors are locked behind us," said Cornwall.

"But the king will be trapped out there," said Gloucester.

"That's an order," said Cornwall. "It's going to be a rough night."

The heavens opened and the rain fell, heavy as hammer blows. Kent hunched up against it, peering through the pelting gloom for any sign of Lear. At last, there was a great flash of lightning and Kent saw the old man:

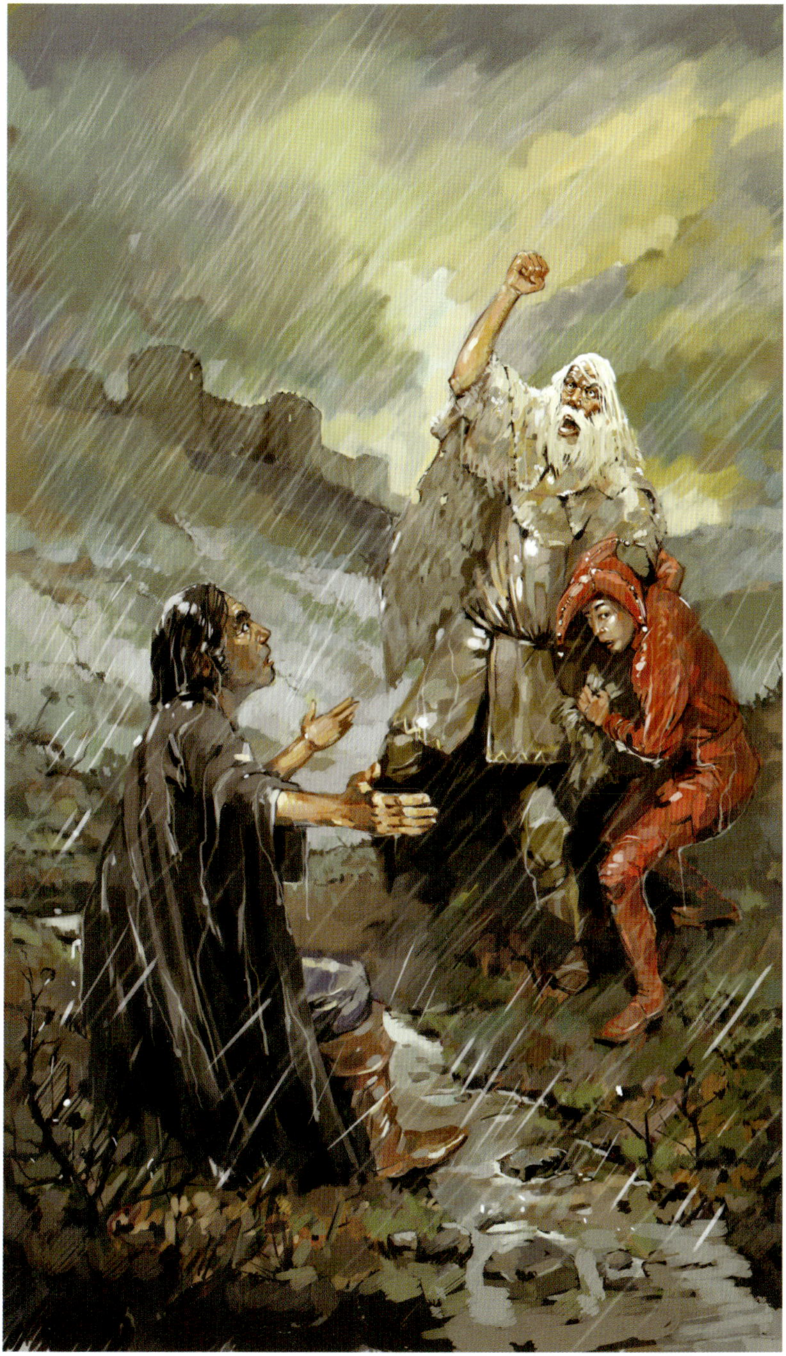

he was already drenched, his fine clothes ruined, his great white beard sodden and bedraggled. Still he was striding about and waving his arms, roaring and raving into the face of the storm.

"You call this a wind?" cried Lear. "Blow stronger! You, thunder, clap louder! I want you to deafen me! Is this the best you can do, rain? Come on – my daughters have treated me far worse than you, and I gave them everything I had!"

Kent saw that the Fool was trying to drag Lear into a little shack that stood nearby, but the old man went on as if he wasn't there. "Bring me a flood," he roared, "to drown the world and sweep away all the ungrateful fiends that say they love their father and lie!"

"Come, sir," shouted Kent as he tried to make himself heard, "this storm is too harsh. Let's take shelter until it has passed."

"Oh Cordelia, what have I done?" wailed Lear, and he sank to his knees in the mud. He looked up at Kent, exhausted suddenly, as if the storm inside himself had blown itself out. He turned to the Fool, who was soaked to the skin.

"Are you cold, boy?" Lear asked, suddenly gentle. The Fool nodded. "Oh, I'm sorry. Come on, let's get out of the rain."

Lear got up, took the Fool by the hand and at last led him into the shack.

Gloucester kept pacing; he couldn't sleep.

"Did you see how Goneril and Regan treated their father?" he said. "Letting him go off into that terrible storm? Heaven knows what's happened to him!"

"It's awful," said Edmund.

"Well I've had enough," said Gloucester. "I'm going to go and look for him myself. Before I do …" At last he stopped pacing, and took a deep breath. "I shouldn't really tell you this. If anyone found out, it would cost me my life, so you mustn't breathe a word at all."

"Of course not, Father," said Edmund, but to himself he thought, *you are making it so easy for me to destroy you!*

Gloucester unlocked a draw and pulled a letter from it.

"I'm not the only one who thinks Goneril and Regan can't be trusted to look after their father," said Gloucester. "Read this. You'll see I'm in contact with powerful people in France." Edmund knew he meant Cordelia and her husband the king. "Once they hear what's happened to him tonight they'll come and save him – and the country."

So you're a worthless traitor are you, Father? thought Edmund. *And you've even given me proof of it. Well, don't worry, I shall take this straight to Cornwall. He'll see you hang for it, and then I shall become the Earl of Gloucester as I have always deserved to be.*

But all that he said was, "You can count on me, Father."

CHAPTER FIVE
The Lowest of the Low

The roof of the shack was full of holes and the rain poured in, but at least its thick walls protected them from the wind, and Kent was far happier to be inside than out on the moor.

"How could they?" Lear kept muttering, and then, "After everything I did for them! No, if I think about that any more I'll go mad." He shook his head and looked thoughtfully around the shack. "How long have I been king of this country? Yet not in all those years have I been in a place like this. What must it be like to be poor, to live your whole life at the mercy of the elements, with no food

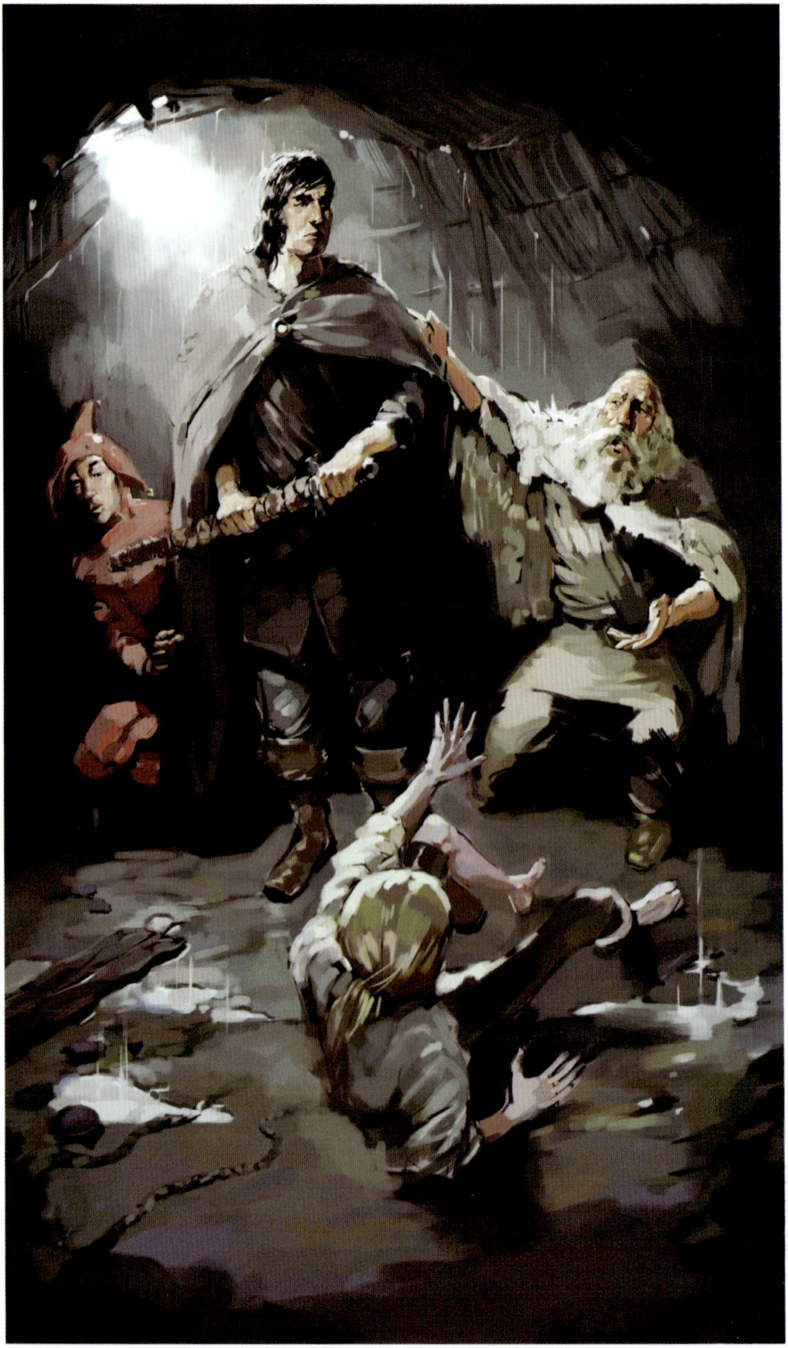

to eat, no warm place to shelter? To have *nothing*." That word made Lear stop to think for a moment. "A king should be ashamed to have lived so long and not thought about this until now!"

Something stirred in the shadows.

"Who's that?" cried the Fool.

Kent drew his sword, but put it away again when he saw that it was just a harmless beggar who'd been sleeping there.

None of them recognised the twisted and filthy young man as Gloucester's elder son.

"Poor Tom," said Edgar. "Pity Poor Tom, he's cold. Oh yes! The devils chased him through the wilderness, they did! They put daggers under his pillow and hid poison in his food!"

"What's that?" said Lear.

"Ignore him," said Kent. "The poor fellow's mad."

"Mad is he?" said Lear. "Then he must have given his kingdom to his daughters — that'd drive anyone mad."

"This cold night will turn us all into fools and madmen," said the Fool, shivering.

Lear looked at Edgar, who had only a little blanket to cover himself.

"No, he's here to teach us all a lesson," Lear said. "To show us that, for all his pride and pomp, a man is just a weak, naked, trembling animal like this – even if he was born a king!"

Suddenly, Lear started to tear off his clothes. "Nothing!" he cried. "Nothing! Nothing!" Kent and the Fool rushed over to stop him.

"I wouldn't do that if I were you," said the Fool. "You can see it's not a good night for a swim."

"Who's in here?" It was Gloucester's voice. He came in, carrying a torch. "There you are, sire! I'm so glad to have found you!"

Edgar was scared his father would recognise him, so he went into his mad act.

"The devils are back!" he cried, pointing at Gloucester's torch. "Burning devils! Poor Tom has eaten lizards and cow dung! They beat him and threw him into prison!"

As Edgar hoped, his father looked away from him in disgust.

"Don't waste your time with this lunatic, sire, I beg of you," said Gloucester. "Come with me, I have a little house you can rest in; it's not much, but it's better than this."

"No," said Lear. "I have already been taught a great lesson by this young man – I want to hear more of his wisdom."

"Fee fie foe fum!" babbled Edgar. "I smell the blood of a British man!"

"We have to get the king to that house of yours," said Kent to Gloucester. "His nerves are shredded. He must be frozen. Much more of this and he'll go mad for sure."

"Can you blame him?" said Gloucester. "His daughters sent him out into the storm to die. No father can know that and not go a little bit mad. I understand: my beloved son plotted to kill me."

The breath caught in Gloucester's throat. Edgar could see that his father was on the verge of tears.

"Poor Tom's cold!" Edgar muttered.

"You should rest," Kent said.

"I am fine," said Gloucester. "Oh, but I do wish my friend Kent was here. He told me there were bad times coming and he got out of the country before it was too late."

Kent was about to reach out and comfort Gloucester, to tell him the truth, and then thought better of it. "Let the king bring his new friend, the lunatic," he said, "and let's all go now."

"He is not going to get away with this," said Cornwall, once he'd read Gloucester's letter from Cordelia. "I'll take care of him before we leave here. You have done well."

"I only wish it hadn't been me who'd told you," said Edmund.

"You are a good son," said Cornwall. "It can't have been easy to condemn your father to death – even if it was the right thing to do. Your reward is to be the new Earl of Gloucester."

It took all Edmund's strength not to grin with triumph. He had to look serious; he was an important man now.

"If the letter is correct, the French intend to invade us," Edmund said. "War is coming."

"I look forward to it," said Cornwall.

The little house Gloucester had provided for them was warm and comfortable. Gloucester had gone off to get them some food, but Kent could see that it was already too late. After all the heartbreak and disappointment he had endured, Lear had lost his mind.

Kent watched the old king and the madman Poor Tom conducting a make-believe trial of Goneril and Regan. From the way Lear acted, it was clear that he actually thought that his daughters were standing in front of him – and that he still had the power to punish them!

Gloucester returned without food, and Kent could see from the look on his face that something terrible had happened.

"What is it?" Kent asked.

"We haven't much time," Gloucester whispered. "I've just had word that Cornwall and the rest are plotting to have the king murdered."

"What?" Kent couldn't believe his ears. "The king? Their father? Look at him, he's a harmless old man! How can he possibly pose any threat to them now!"

"You think they care?" said Gloucester. "They have hearts of granite. No, you must get him out of here as quickly as you can. I've arranged transport for you. No one will expect to find the king in the back of this old farmer's cart, so Cornwall's soldiers won't bother to search it. Take him to Dover: his daughter Cordelia has just landed there with a French army. She'll be able to protect him and, by the gods, drive her wicked sisters out of Britain forever!"

It was so much to take in all at once; for a moment Kent just stood there.

"Well go on then," said Gloucester. "They are coming; a few minutes could make all the difference."

Kent got the king and his Fool into the cart Gloucester had provided. He gathered as many of Lear's knights as he could find to guard them on their journey.

"Come on then," he said to Gloucester. "You can't stay here. If they find out you helped us get away, there'll be hell to pay."

"This castle has been my family's home for centuries," Gloucester replied. "I couldn't just abandon it to those villains – that's what a coward would do. Besides, I still have one loyal son: my dear Edmund. You just make sure the king reaches Dover. Don't worry about me."

"As you wish," said Kent. He was very worried for his old friend, but he knew Gloucester could not be persuaded, so he nodded and walked away.

Gloucester had sounded so brave, he'd almost convinced himself that he wasn't afraid; but when he looked down at his hands, he saw they were shaking.

CHAPTER SIX
Blinded

Oswald brought the news that Lear had escaped. He smiled when he saw how angry it made Cornwall.

"The traitor Gloucester!" he cried. "This is all his doing."

"Hang him!" said Regan.

"Tear out his eyes!" said Goneril.

"Bring him to me," Cornwall ordered his guards. When they had gone, he turned to Edmund. "You won't want to watch this. Take Goneril here back to her castle. She'll need your protection on the journey; these are violent times and you can't trust anyone."

"Yes, my lord," said Edmund and he bowed and followed Goneril out of the room.

Gloucester was in the library when Cornwall's soldiers found him. He was too proud to hide from them and realised that there was nothing to be gained by resisting. He knew, though, that he had to give Lear and the others plenty of time to get away, so when he was dragged before Cornwall and Regan, he tried playing innocent.

"My lord, Princess," he said, "my friends – I don't understand what is going on."

"Liar," sneered Regan.

"Tie him to that chair," said Cornwall.

"If I have done anything wrong," said Gloucester as the soldiers pulled the ropes tight around his arms and legs, "please tell me what it is and I will put it right, I swear I will."

"You are a filthy traitor," said Regan.

"How could you say such a thing, Princess?" said Gloucester. "I am nothing of the kind."

Regan reached out and tore a handful of hair from his beard. Gloucester cried out.

"What are you doing?" he said. "You can't treat me like this!"

"You are conspiring with the enemies of the state," said Cornwall. "We can do absolutely anything we like."

"Where have you sent the king?" asked Regan furiously.

"I don't know what you're talking about," said Gloucester.

"We have the letter," said Cornwall. "The letter from Cordelia."

Gloucester's heart sank. There was no point pretending any longer. They knew that he had been in contact with Cordelia and the French. They could hang him for that.

"I sent the king to Dover," he said. "To the one daughter who truly loves him."

"Why?" asked Regan.

"Because I didn't want to see you get your monstrous claws into him, or watch your sister sink her fangs in his royal flesh!" Gloucester roared suddenly. "But I tell you one thing I will see – and that is his revenge on the whole vicious lot of you!"

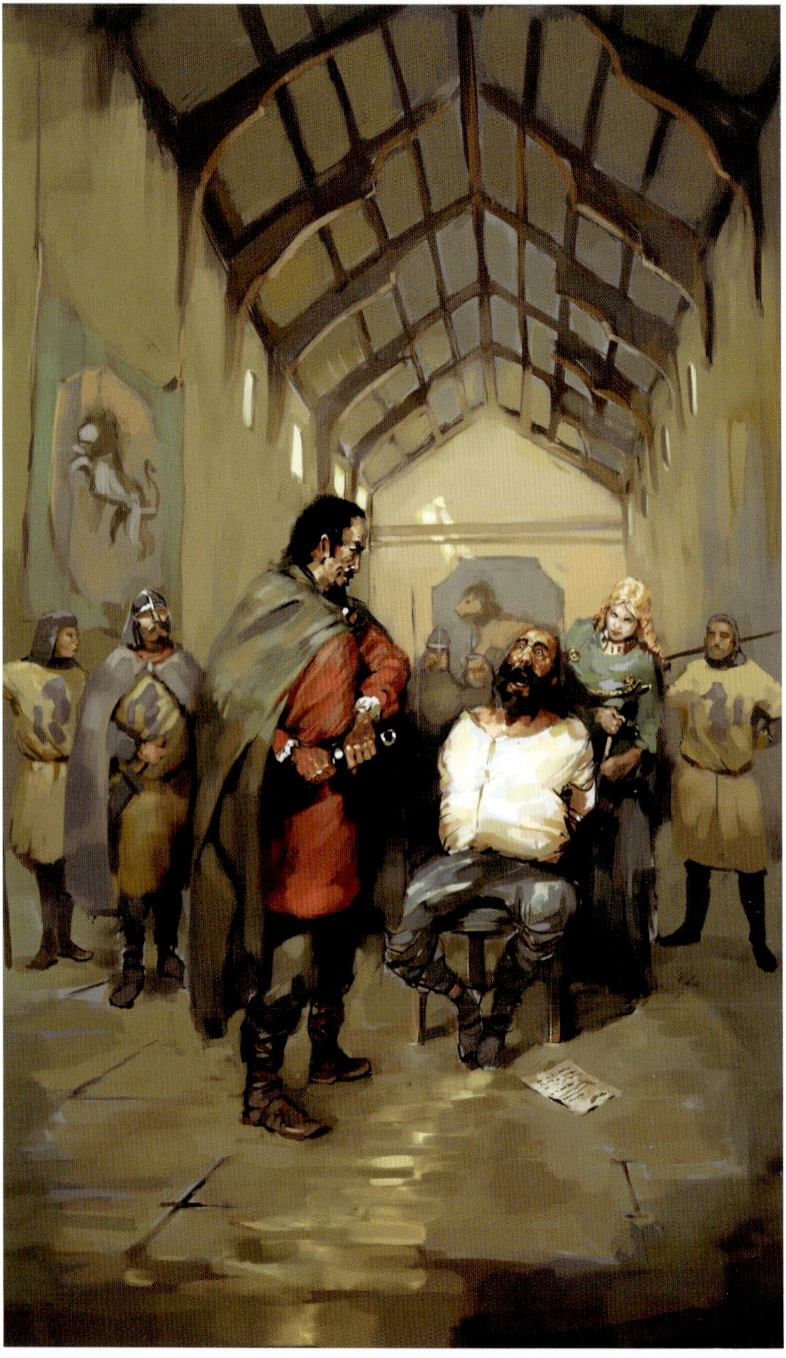

"Oh you won't *see* it, old man," said Cornwall. "Hold the chair!"

Gloucester struggled to free himself as Cornwall approached him, but Cornwall's soldiers held the chair firmly. With one hand, Cornwall pulled Gloucester's right eye open; with the other he drew his dagger.

"No, no please! Help me, somebody!" was all Gloucester managed to say before he screamed in such agony that it made even the soldiers feel sick.

For a moment, Regan looked closely at Gloucester's face and the blood pouring from his empty eye socket. "Well that's no good, putting out just one of them," she said. "He's lopsided now."

"You think of everything, my love," said Cornwall. He held open Gloucester's left eye and was raising his dagger again when one of his soldiers cried out, "That's enough!"

The soldier sprang at Cornwall, dragging him off Gloucester.

"How dare you, you dog!" said Cornwall, wrestling himself free.

"My lord, I have followed you since I was a child – and fought with you in many a terrible battle – but I will not stand for this wanton cruelty!" said the soldier.

"Then you will die," said Cornwall, lashing out at him with his dagger. The soldier dodged out of the way and drew his sword.

Cornwall fought well, but the soldier was quicker and stronger, and soon he thrust his blade into Cornwall's belly.

"Is not one of you going to protect your master?" Regan screamed at the other soldiers. They did not move. "Then I will!"

She grabbed a sword and stabbed the soldier in the back. He sank to the floor.

"Forgive me my lord," the soldier said to Gloucester, "but at least you still have one eye to see this villain punished," and with that, he died.

"It's the last thing you will see!" said Cornwall, dragging himself to his feet. "Out, vile jelly!"

Gloucester gave another terrible cry.

"Edmund!" he called. "My loyal son! May you avenge your poor father!"

Cornwall had lost a lot of blood and he was very weak, but he still had the strength to laugh in Gloucester's face.

"Edmund?" he said. "You're pinning your hopes on *Edmund?* Who do you think gave us the letter? Who do you think told us you were a traitor? Edmund hates you, old man, and he wants you dead."

Cornwall's words hurt even more than his dagger.

"Then …" said Gloucester, "then it was my poor Edgar who was true to me all along."

"How funny!" cackled Regan. "It's only now, when you're blind, that you finally *see* the truth!"

"Untie him," said Cornwall, "and turn him out of the house. He's no threat to us now. Let him wander blindly in the world until he dies, as a warning to anyone else who might dare stand up against us."

Cornwall staggered, and Regan only just caught him.

"Fetch a doctor," she said. "My husband is wounded!"

Edgar had thought of following the king to Dover, but he couldn't leave his father behind. He was still trying to get into the castle to help him escape when the great gates swung open and he saw Gloucester stumble out, with bloody rags bandaging his face. The sight broke Edgar's heart.

"Oh Father, what have they done to you?" he said. Then he saw the old man lose his footing and trip over, and he ran to him.

"Let me help you, sir," said Edgar. "Yes, yes. Help you."

"I know your voice," Gloucester replied. "You're that poor mad beggar fellow from last night."

"Who else would I be?" said Edgar. "Tell me that!"

"You reminded me of my poor son Edgar," said Gloucester. "I'm glad you're not him. After all the terrible, stupid things I did, I would be ashamed to meet him again."

"No, no," said Edgar, doing all he could to stop himself from crying.

"Don't upset yourself," said Gloucester. "Don't you understand that the gods are just like wicked little boys playing with flies? They kill us for the fun of it!"

"Is there nothing I can do for you?" said Edgar in despair.

"One thing," said Gloucester. "Take me to the edge of the tallest cliff in Dover and leave me there. I won't need anyone to guide me after that. If you do it, you'll be well paid, I promise."

He's going to jump off, thought Edgar. *My poor father wants to kill himself!* He tried to stay calm. "Come on then," he said, and they set off, arm in arm.

"So this is what the world has come to – " said Gloucester, "the mad leading the blind."

CHAPTER SEVEN
Enemies

Oswald was not having a good day. He had returned to Goneril's castle to bring a message to her husband, Albany. He was expecting to be rewarded with a coin for bringing the good news about the capture of the traitor Gloucester. Instead, Albany was outraged. He even *smiled* when Oswald told him that the French army had landed!

Oswald told Goneril all this when she and Edmund finally arrived back from Gloucester's castle. He could see from the way Goneril couldn't take her eyes off Edmund that she had fallen in love with him.

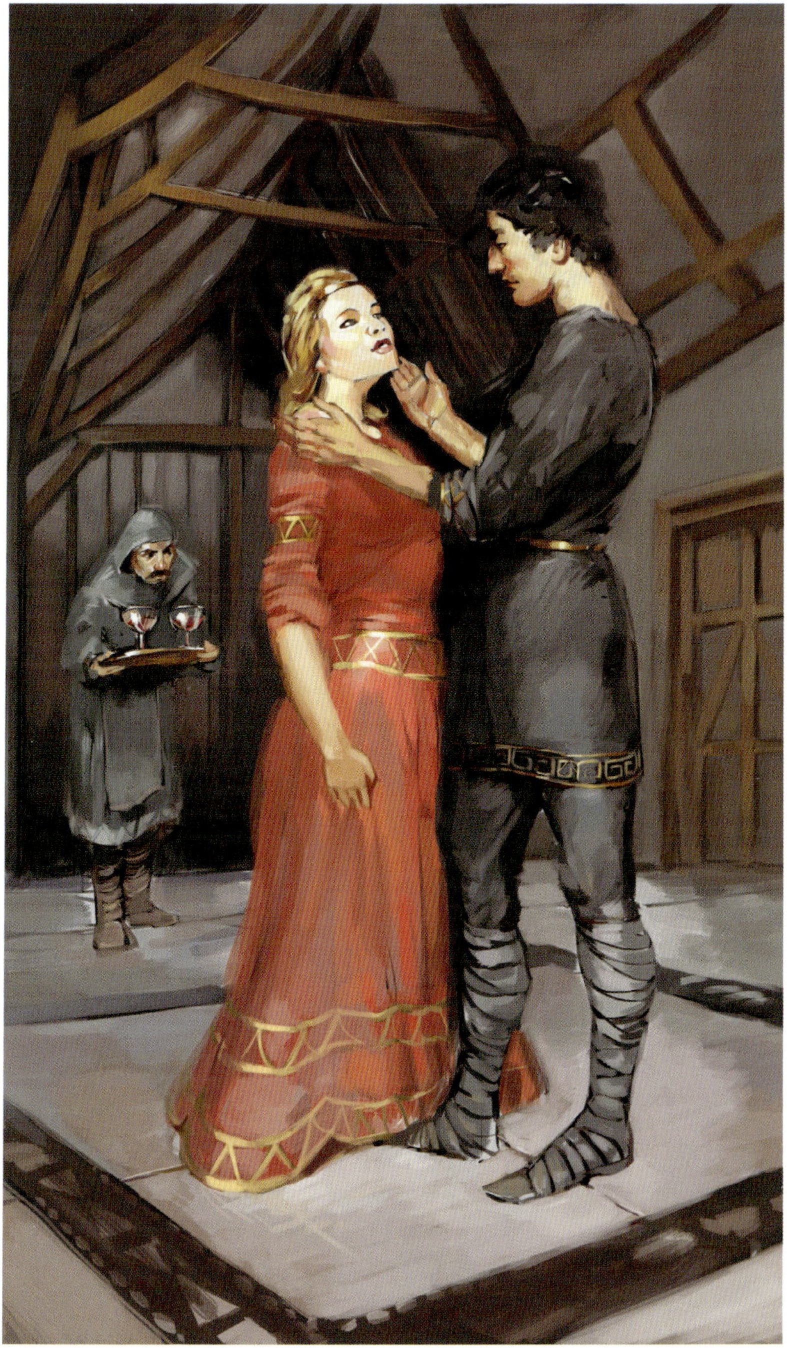

No wonder, thought Oswald, *with a husband like she's got!*

"Thank you for protecting me on the journey," Goneril said to Edmund. "Now I think you should return to my sister and her husband. Cornwall will need your help as he prepares for war against the French. But I will miss you!"

"Princess," said Edmund, "I am yours until death."

His lips were so close to hers, she knew he wanted to kiss her as much as she wanted to kiss him … But there were servants watching and she didn't want to give the castle gossips any more to chatter about, so instead she just said, "Travel safely."

"I will," said Edmund.

Goneril stood and watched Edmund ride off. When, at long last, he had vanished into the far distance, she sighed, and went to find her husband.

Albany was in the great hall of the castle. He'd been drinking.

"There you are," Goneril said coldly. "I thought you might come and welcome me home after my long journey."

"You, madam!" Albany sneered. "Ha!"

"I don't know what I've done to be talked to like that!" said Goneril.

"What you've done?" said Albany. "You've only treated your dear father, the king himself, so badly that he's gone mad – that's all! Never mind everything he's given you – and that fiend Cornwall! What kind of monster are you?"

"What kind of coward are you?" Goneril snapped. "The French are on our soil, led by that traitor, my sister Cordelia. They are getting ready to take this country away from us and, instead of mustering our troops and preparing our strategy, you're sitting here doing nothing!"

"Have you looked at yourself?" Albany cried. "There is nothing so ugly as a beautiful woman who has turned to evil."

"Fool," said Goneril.

"If I weren't so noble I'd come over there and tear you to pieces!" said Albany.

"You're too much of a coward to do it!" Goneril cried.

It looked like Albany was going to throw his cup at her when Oswald strode in.

"My lord, another messenger has just arrived," said Oswald.

"What's the news?" Albany asked.

"The Duke of Cornwall is dead, my lord," said Oswald.

"Dead?" gasped Goneril.

"Murdered by a common soldier," said Oswald, "while he was blinding the Earl of Gloucester."

"*Blinding* him?" Albany couldn't believe his ears. "The great and noble Gloucester! What has he ever done to anyone? What about Edmund, Gloucester's son – what does he think about all this?"

"It was Edmund who told the Duke of Cornwall about his father's treachery," said Oswald.

"That's terrible!" said Goneril. For once she seemed truly upset.

"It's a bit late to be showing a flicker of conscience now!" Albany said.

"That's not what I mean, you idiot!" said Goneril. "It's terrible because my sister Regan is now a widow. I've just sent Edmund back to her. What if he marries *her*, instead of—"

Albany closed his eyes and smiled bitterly. "Instead of marrying you, you mean? I suppose I was going to meet with a nasty accident, was that it? Serves me right for getting in your way."

Goneril didn't answer.

"You can go to him for all I care," said Albany. "From the sound of it, you've already made up your mind."

In Dover Harbour, under a bright summer sun, the French king stood aboard his ship and bade farewell to Cordelia, his beloved wife.

"Do you have to go?" she asked him.

"Yes, my dearest," the king replied. "There is talk of rebellion at home. Some people think I'm so in love with you that I am ignoring my homeland. If I show myself in Paris and throw a banquet for them, they will be reassured and then I can return to you and we can take back this country from those monstrous sisters of yours."

"I shall miss you," said Cordelia.

"And I you," said the king, "but it won't be for long. I had wanted to pay my respects to your father before I left. How is he? The Earl of Kent brought him to Dover more than a week ago, and yet we still have not seen him."

"Kent has come to see me," said Cordelia. "He tells me my father has good days and bad days."

"But surely he must want to see you," said the king.

"Kent says that on the bad days he wouldn't know who I am, and on the good days …" Cordelia paused, trying not to cry, "on the good days, when he can remember, he is so ashamed of what he did to me that he can't bear to face me."

"I need you to be strong," said the king, putting his arms around Cordelia, "to show leadership to my army when I'm not here."

"Of course," said Cordelia. "I'm sorry."

"Now I must go," said the king. "It is time."

"Hurry back to me," said Cordelia. "The enemy will be here soon."

When at last her husband's ship was far out to sea, Cordelia walked back through the French camp, past many thousands of soldiers sharpening their weapons, cleaning their armour and preparing for battle.

Soldiers crowded the road to Regan's palace – so many of them that Oswald thought he'd never get through.

He had to keep saying, "I carry an important message from Princess Goneril!" and only then would they grumble and get out of his way.

When at last he made it to the palace, he was met by Regan herself.

"Are my sister's troops ready for battle?" she asked.

"Princess, they are," Oswald replied.

"You have a message there," Regan said. "Give it to me."

"Forgive me," said Oswald, "but my mistress, your sister, told me I had to give it to Lord Edmund personally."

"He's not here," said Regan. "Oh, it was such a mistake of my dead husband to let old Gloucester go after he'd blinded him! He should have just killed him to get rid of him – but, oh no, he thought the sight of that eyeless idiot would be a warning to others! Instead of that, anyone who sees him stumbling blindly around feels sorry for the old fool and blames us for being so mean to him! I'd laugh at their stupidity, but it could make all the difference in the battle, so I've sent Edmund off to find his father and get rid of him once and for all."

"Then I must go after him," said Oswald.

"It's too dangerous," said Regan. "You should stay here until after the battle."

"I have my orders," said Oswald. "I must find Lord Edmund."

"Is it really so important?" said Regan. "Here, give me the message. Let me read it," and she reached out to take the letter.

"I cannot," said Oswald. "Forgive me, lady, but my mistress was very clear: the message is for Edmund and no one else. Not even you."

Regan scowled.

"How stupid do you think I am?" she said. "We both know my sister wants to marry Edmund. That's what the message is about."

Oswald tried not to give anything away, but it was obvious from his expression that Regan was right.

"Then let me save you a trip," said Regan. "My sister is still married and I'm not any more, so Edmund has decided he'd rather marry me. We've talked about it and he's agreed."

"My mistress will want to know this as soon as possible," said Oswald.

"I bet she will," said Regan. "You should hurry back to her."

"Good day, Princess," said Oswald.

"Oh, and Oswald?" said Regan.

"Yes, Princess?" said Oswald.

"If you see that old blind Gloucester on your travels," said Regan, "be a darling, will you, and kill him. It would be the perfect wedding present for his son and me."

CHAPTER EIGHT
The Great Fall

Edgar and his father Gloucester had reached Dover at last. The old man could no longer see, but he could smell the salt air and hear the cries of the seagulls that wheeled overhead.

"We're here, aren't we?" he said.

"Yes, sir, we are, yes," Edgar jabbered in his Poor Tom voice.

"And you have brought me to the very top of the tallest cliff as you promised?" said Gloucester.

"Promised, yes, promised," said Edgar – though in fact they were nowhere near the cliffs and the ground before them was covered in soft grass.

"Are you sure?" said Gloucester. Perhaps he'd caught a note of doubt in Edgar's voice. "The ground seems very flat."

"Oh, no, sir!" said Edgar. "It's steep – horrible steep! Can't you feel it? It makes me dizzy, standing up here so high. The birds in the air below us look no bigger than beetles, and, oh, those fishermen all the way down there on the beach, they're as small as mice! No, I'd like to go now. I'm scared I might fall."

"You can go," said Gloucester, "but leave me here. I promised you a reward, so here," Gloucester fumbled in his pocket, "take this purse of money, and my thanks. Goodbye."

"Goodbye, sir," said Edgar, but he stayed exactly where he was. "The gods bless you," he said in a quieter voice, so Gloucester would think he was walking away.

Gloucester waited a few moments until he thought he was alone. Then he took a deep breath and jumped forward – landing face down in the soft grass in front of him.

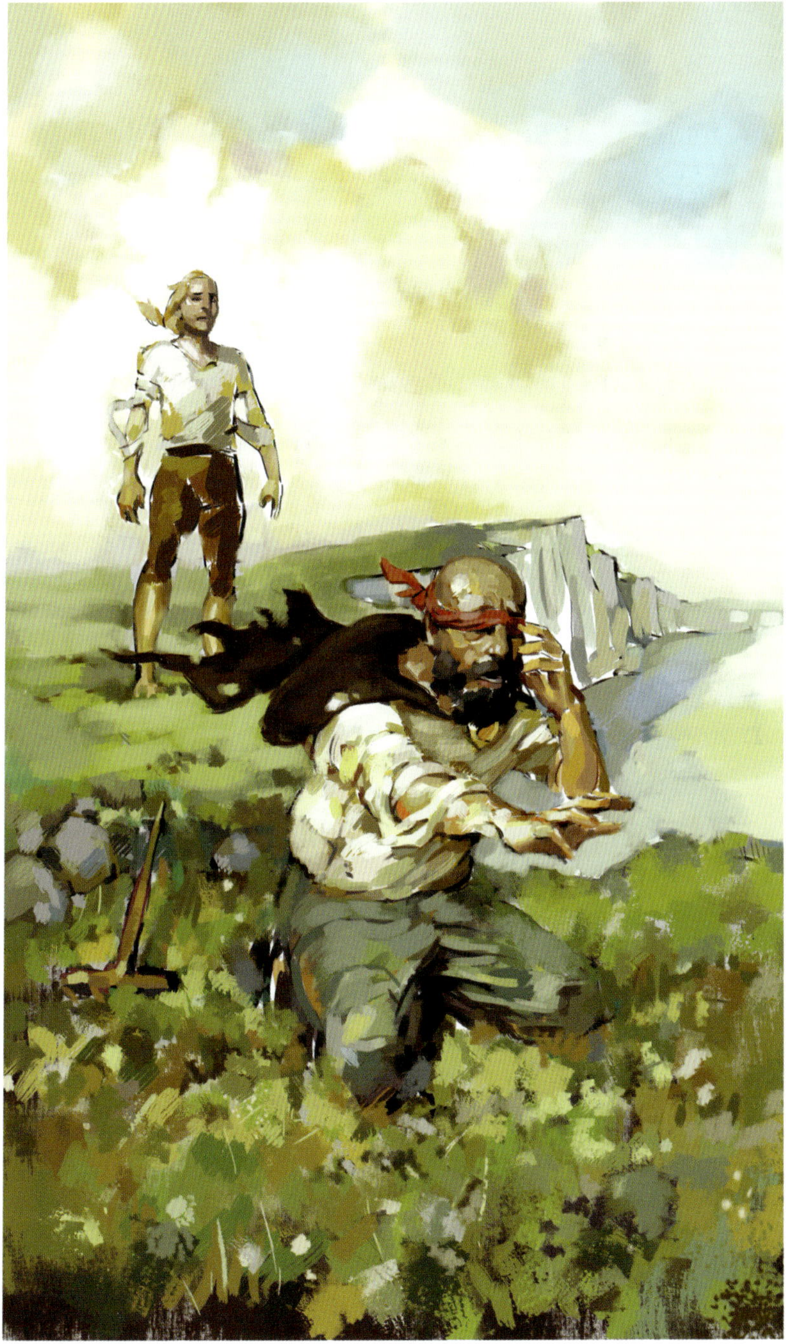

Before the old man had a chance to think about what had just happened to him, Edgar cried out, "It's a miracle!" He no longer used his Poor Tom voice because he wanted his blind father to think he was now someone else, a passer-by. "I wouldn't have believed it if I hadn't seen it with my own eyes!" he went on. "Are you all right there, sir?"

"Go away and let me die," groaned Gloucester.

"'*Die*'? he says!" Edgar chuckled. "Sir, I have just watched you fall from the tallest cliff in Dover and land here on the ground a hundred feet below, with not a mark on you! If that fall couldn't kill you, I don't know what could!"

"There must be some mistake," said Gloucester. "That beggar man; he tricked me!"

"What beggar man, sir?" said Edgar. "I saw no beggar man. Oh no – the fellow with you looked more like some kind of spirit. You know, like something not of this world!"

"There was something about his voice,"

said Gloucester. "I thought it reminded me of my son."

"Perhaps the gods sent him," said Edgar. "Yes, that must be it – to protect you. They surely want you to live."

"Then I suppose I must," said Gloucester, with a sigh.

They heard singing, and Edgar turned to see a mad old man in ragged clothes with a crown of wild flowers on his head. *Another Bedlam beggar*, he thought. *Poor souls! This world is full of them!*

As the old beggar came closer, Edgar realised who it was.

"Oh dear gods!" Edgar said.

"I know that voice," said Gloucester. "Isn't it the king?"

"Every inch a king!" said Lear as he danced towards them. "I only have to look at a man and he'll tremble out of fear of my great power!" Lear pulled a serious face, and then burst out laughing. "Though it turns out all the power in the world isn't enough to stop you going mad."

"Let me kiss your hand," said Gloucester.

"Ooh, let me wipe it first," said Lear, sniffing his hand suspiciously. "It smells of death."

"Do you remember me?" Gloucester asked.

Lear looked blankly at Gloucester for a moment, and then a tear rolled down his cheek.

"I remember your eyes," he said. "Do you see how this world works, blind man?"

"I see it feelingly," said Gloucester.

"A farmer's dog barks at a beggar," said Lear, "so the beggar runs away – and that's all there is to it. The more people you can scare, the 'greater' you are. If a dog could frighten everyone, we'd make him king! You're Gloucester, aren't you?"

"Yes, sire," said Gloucester.

"Don't cry, Gloucester," said Lear. "This a mad world, where only the insane talk sense, and only the blind can truly see. That's why we cry when we are born – because we know we have come to this great stage of fools."

Edgar almost couldn't bear to watch as

Lear embraced his loyal old friend and kissed him. He was wiping the tears from his eyes just as a platoon of French soldiers began to surround them.

"Your Majesty," said the commanding officer, kneeling before Lear, "your royal daughter, Cordelia, has sent us to take you to her."

"Are you going to lock me up?" said Lear.

"No, sir," said the officer, "but the time for battle is drawing near and she is worried you might be taken prisoner by your enemies if we do not protect you."

"You could ransom me if you like," said Lear. "You'd make a fortune. I'm a king, you know."

"I know, and I obey you, sire," said the officer, bowing.

"Then you'd better get a move on," said Lear.

"'Get a move on', Your Majesty?" said the officer.

"Yes, or you'll never catch me!" said Lear and he ran off, laughing.

"After him!" the officer ordered his men. "There isn't much time."

"Is battle close then?" asked Edgar.

"The enemy is on its way and travelling fast," said the officer. "They could be anywhere around here. That's why Queen Cordelia was so eager we find her father and take him to safety. You'll get going too if you know what's good for you," and he went off after his troops.

"Thank you, we shall," said Edgar. "Come, sir, let's go and find a safe place."

Oswald couldn't believe his luck. Regan had told him that if he found Gloucester and killed him he'd be well rewarded; and now, on his way back to Goneril's castle whom should he see but Gloucester! There were soldiers with him, so Oswald hid behind some bushes until they'd gone and Gloucester had no one to protect him except some mad-looking fellow in rags.

"Prepare to die, you traitor!" Oswald cried, springing out at Gloucester with his sword drawn.

Gloucester didn't try to defend himself; on the contrary, he stood still waiting for the blade. Just before Oswald could strike, though, the man in rags jumped on him. The two of them rolled around on the ground, wrestling for control of the sword.

"Unhand me, villain!" Oswald growled – and then he felt the cold steel slide into his belly and tasted blood in his mouth.

"Is he dead?" asked Gloucester.

"Yes," said Edgar.

"Shame," said Gloucester, sinking down by a tree. "I thought he'd come to set me free."

The twisted trunk was sharp against his back, and the ground hard beneath him, but suddenly the old man was filled with a great feeling of peace.

Edgar grabbed the bag Oswald had been carrying and found inside the message that Goneril had told him to deliver only to Edmund. "My darling love," it said. "Remember how you promised to kill my husband, Albany? Please do it soon, so that we can be married!"

Oh, my brother – how could you have fallen so far? Edgar thought, but he tucked the letter into his pocket. He knew it would come in useful.

"Come, sir, let's go," he said to Gloucester, but when he reached over to take his father's hand, it was cold; Gloucester was dead.

In his tent in the French camp in Dover, Kent looked at himself in the mirror. He was washed, dressed in his own clothes and even his beard was growing back. There was no need for disguise any more, and it felt good to be himself again.

The sun was high in the sky. It was noon: time to go and see Cordelia.

"How is he?" Cordelia asked.

"Asleep," said Kent. "You must remember that he has been through a lot. You can't expect him still to be the father that you once knew."

"Thank you, dear Kent," said Cordelia, "for everything you have done for him."

Kent nodded, and gave a sign to the servants that it was time. They brought Lear into Cordelia's tent on a litter. He was fast asleep.

"I wish there was medicine in my kiss," said Cordelia, "so that this would heal all the wounds he has suffered at my sisters' hands."

Cordelia knelt down and kissed her father. His eyes flickered, then opened and he stared at her a moment and shook his head. "Are you an angel?" he said, and Cordelia shook her head. "You shouldn't have taken me out of my grave," said Lear. "You are a soul in bliss, but I am bound upon a wheel of fire so that my tears scald me like molten lead."

"Poor father," said Cordelia.

"Don't make fun of me," said Lear, "I'm a foolish old man. I think I should know you – and this gentleman. You look like my daughter Cordelia. Do you have poison for me? You should have, after everything I've done to you."

"No, no," said Cordelia, trying very hard not to cry. "Will you walk with me, sire? Please."

Painfully, Lear got to his feet. Cordelia slid her arm through his and Kent watched them walk off, talking quietly to each other.

CHAPTER NINE
War

Edmund had everything he had ever wanted. He had wanted to be Earl of Gloucester, and now he was. He had wanted to be a great power in the land, and now he commanded the mighty army that was preparing to fight Cordelia and the French for control of Britain. He had wanted to be loved by beautiful and important women, and now two of the king's daughters – Goneril *and* Regan – both wanted to marry him!

So why did *having* feel so much less exciting than *wanting*?

It certainly didn't help that the Duke of

Albany, who was supposed to be on his side, hadn't yet arrived with any of his soldiers. *The fat idiot!* Edmund worried that he'd found out that Goneril was in love with him. Regan certainly went on about it enough!

"For the hundredth time," Edmund snapped when Regan asked him about it yet again, "I do not love your sister!"

"Because I'd rather lose this battle", said Regan, "than lose you," and she made that silly 'love' face of hers and wrapped herself around him again.

Well I wouldn't! Edmund thought. *I'd drop you like a shot if it meant that I'd end up King of Britain!* Though all he said was, "I love you too, darling."

He couldn't marry them both, of course. In all honesty, he preferred Goneril, but she was married to Albany, and Albany had a large army so he needed Albany's help to defeat Cordelia. Of course, he and Goneril could always poison Albany once the battle was won. If Albany ever turned up, that is!

A trumpet sounded.

Edmund's most loyal captain entered his tent and bowed.

"My lord Edmund," he said, "Princess Goneril and her husband, the Duke of Albany, have arrived."

"At long last!" cried Edmund.

Riding in with Goneril at his side, Albany didn't look particularly happy to be there. He climbed down from his horse but wouldn't shake Edmund's outstretched hand.

"Let's not pretend that we like one another," Albany said, "but this is an invasion by a foreign army and I would ally myself with the devil himself –" Albany looked Edmund straight in the eye as he said this, "– if that was what I had to do to defend my country."

Edmund said nothing, but thought about what poison he would use to kill Albany. *Anything that gives him a slow, lingering death*, Edmund thought. *He's earned it.*

Edmund's most loyal captain whispered something in his ear.

"The French are in the field," said Edmund. "Let's get this over with."

No one knew how it happened.

Archers loosed clouds of arrows so dense that they darkened the sun. Wave upon wave of French and British horsemen broke upon one another in a fury of steel. Between the foot soldiers there were inspiring acts of great valour and foul crimes of dreadful cruelty. First one army seemed to have the advantage, then the other. Surely the gods would favour the side of right and justice, and punish the wicked.

Surely?

But then the battle was over.

And Cordelia had lost.

Her camp was overrun by Edmund's soldiers, and she and King Lear were brought before their bitterest enemy in chains.

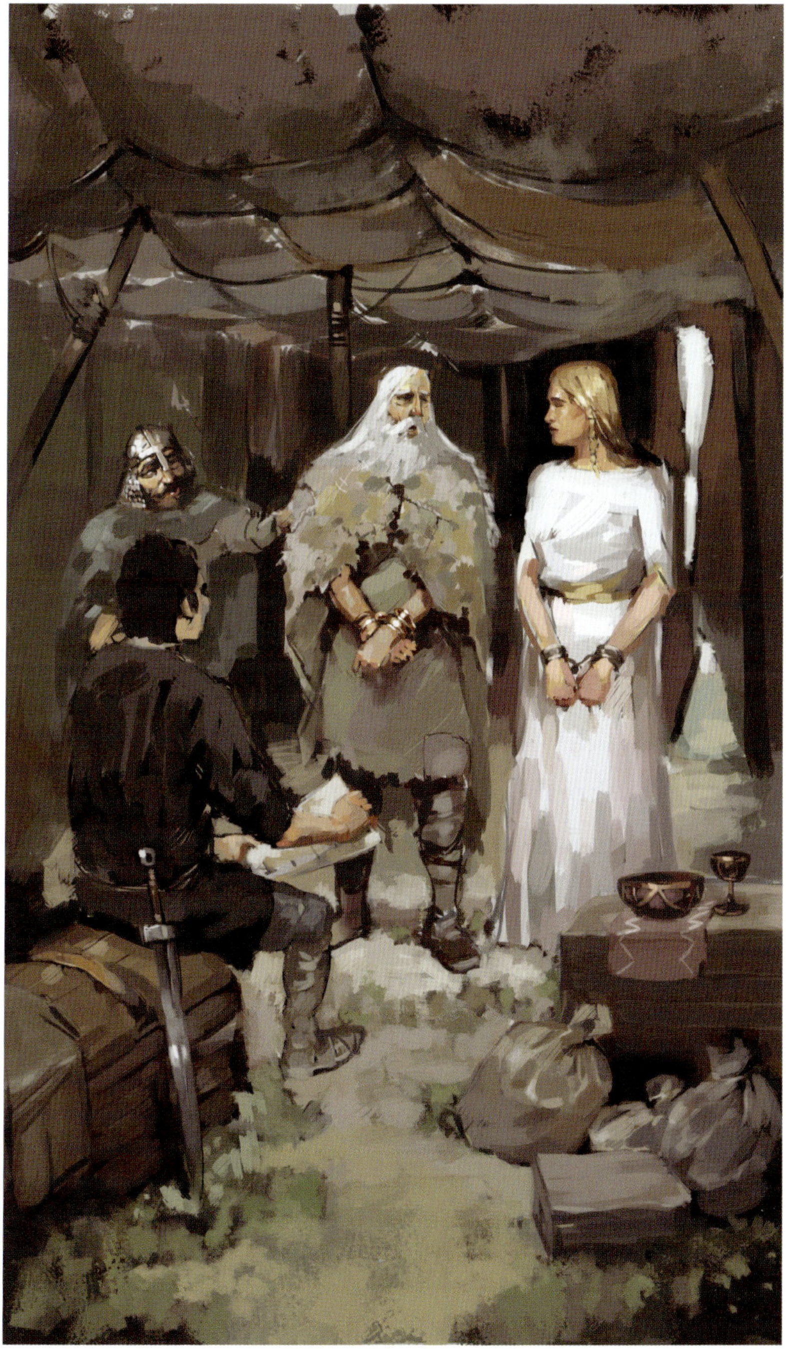

Edmund sneered as he looked them up and down.

"So this is goodness, is it?" he said. "This is majesty? No, this is what happens when you let go of power; this is the reward for your moment of madness, old man." Then he turned to his guards and said, "Take them to prison. We'll decide what to do with them later."

"Oh Father, I'm so sorry," said Cordelia. "I hoped this battle was going to make everything right again, and now all is lost."

"Don't worry," smiled Lear. "In our cell, you and I will sing like birds in a cage. What do we care what people with power do, so long as we have each other to talk and laugh with? Let them live their great lives and do their important deeds! They are nothing compared to two people who truly love one another."

Listening to all this, Edmund felt distinctly unwell.

"Get them out of here!" he commanded. "I think I'm going to retch."

When Lear and Cordelia had been taken away, Edmund signalled to his captain to come over to him. Edmund made sure that no one could overhear as he whispered in the captain's ear, "Follow them to prison and, when you get there, open this letter and do what it tells you."

The captain didn't like the sound of that. If there was nothing wrong with Edmund's orders, why didn't he just tell him what to do – why did he have to write it in a letter?

Edmund saw the captain had his doubts. "This is not the time to start getting soft," he said darkly. "There is no right and wrong any more in this land. Men should do what's in keeping with their times. You don't think that a sword cares who it kills, and these are days of steel."

The captain felt a chill run down his spine. He was in no doubt what would happen to him if he disobeyed his master.

"As you wish, my lord," he said, and left.

Not a moment too soon, thought Edmund as Albany strode in.

"There you are," Albany said rudely.

"Congratulations on a noble victory to you too, my lord," said Edmund sarcastically.

"Never mind all that," said Albany. "What have you done with Lear and Cordelia?"

"I've sent them away to prison," said Edmund. "The fighting has only just finished and everyone's tired. We can decide what to do with them tomorrow, when we're all thinking more clearly. Come, let us go and eat!"

Albany ignored Edmund's invitation.

"My wife and her sister – where are they?" said Albany.

"At supper already," said Edmund. "We should join them."

"I want them brought to us," said Albany.

"Is there something wrong?" Edmund asked. *Does Albany know I plan to poison him?* he thought.

"Just get the women," said Albany.

Edmund had had about enough of Albany's sulking. If it went on much longer, he'd just stab him where he stood.

When Regan and Goneril had arrived, Albany pointed at Edmund and asked, "Which one of you loves this man most?"

"I love him more than eyesight, more than life," said Regan.

"You love nothing and no one but him?" sneered Goneril. "We've heard all this before. Nobody meant it then either."

"I'd show you how dear he is to me," said Regan, "only ..." and she grimaced and clutched her stomach, "only I am feeling most unwell."

"Perhaps you love him so much it's given you indigestion!" snorted Goneril.

"All right then," said Regan, who was clearly in great pain. "Listen to this. Edmund, my love," she went on, taking Edmund's hand, "I want you to know, in front of these people, that I, by my own royal authority, do here declare myself your wife. From now on, everything that I have is yours."

"I won't allow it!" shrieked Goneril.

"That's not for you to decide," said Albany.

"Nor you!" said Edmund.

"Shut your mouth," said Albany furiously. "I've had enough of this. Edmund, Earl of Gloucester, I hereby arrest you on a charge of high treason!"

"What?" cried Edmund. He was outraged.

"Do you really deny all your plotting?" said Albany. "Against me, against Princess Regan here? Against anyone who stands between you and absolute power in this land?"

"Is this true?" said Regan. It looked like Albany's words caused her even more suffering than the pains in her stomach.

"I'm sorry, Regan," said Albany, "but you can't marry him, because he already plans to marry my wife. If you want a husband, you'll have to look elsewhere — if you live long enough."

"What are you talking about?" said Goneril.

"Do you recognise this letter?" said Albany, and he held up the letter that Edgar had taken from Oswald.

"Where did you get that?" asked Goneril.

"Never you mind," said Albany. "It's in your handwriting, isn't it?"

"I've never seen that letter before in my life," said Goneril.

"So you've never called Edmund here your 'darling love'?" said Albany. "Never reminded him of his promise to kill me so that you two can get married?"

"I feel sick!" cried Regan.

"So do I," said Albany.

"That is a lie!" cried Edmund. "I challenge anyone who says otherwise to a duel."

"No, really sick," Regan gasped. She pitched forward. Albany caught her as she fell. She was deathly grey and sweating.

"Princess Regan needs help!" Albany shouted to his servants. "Take her to my tent and look after her."

"To hell with her!" cried Edmund as the servants carried Regan away. "Who dares say that this letter is true?"

"I do."

They looked round. The words had come from a masked stranger who stepped from the shadows.

"Who are you?" asked Edmund.

"My name is for later," said the stranger, drawing his sword. "All you need to know is that I say you are a villain – a traitor to your father, your brother and to this gentleman and that my blade will prove it."

CHAPTER TEN
All for Nothing

Edmund drew his sword and spat at the masked stranger.

"I am Earl of Gloucester," he said, "and by the laws of chivalry, I do not have to fight with dirt like you. I know that my cause is right – and for that reason alone, I will take you on. Remember that when you're face down – pouring your worthless blood into the dirt."

Edmund gave a terrible cry of rage and flew at the stranger. He brought his sword flashing down on the stranger's head – but just in time the stranger ducked out of the way, striking hard at Edmund's undefended arm. Edmund roared with pain and whirled round, slicing and hacking. The stranger expertly parried every blow until it was his turn to drive Edmund back with his relentless attack.

It was a long time since Edmund had fought with anyone of equal skill and the harder he had to fight the angrier he became. Everything had been so easy for him for so long that he felt it was insulting that he should even have to try.

At last, bored by being made to put such an effort into the fight, Edmund decided to finish the stranger with a single, sweeping blow. *This worthless peasant? It'll be like swatting a fly*, Edmund thought. He stood back, swung his arm – and then stopped, surprised by an unfamiliar feeling. Edmund looked down to see the stranger's sword plunged straight into his guts. He felt his fingers grow numb and heard his sword fall and clatter to the ground.

"Edmund!" cried Goneril and she ran to his side as he fell. "What have you done?"

she screamed at Albany.

"Found out the truth it seems," Albany said. "So this is your letter?"

"Of course it is, you animal!" Goneril burst into tears and ran off.

"After her," Albany ordered one of his servants. "In her state of mind, she's capable of anything."

Goneril burst into Albany's tent. Regan lay on his bed, attended by his doctors.

"Forgive me, my lady," said one of them, "but your sister is very ill and needs quiet."

"*Ill?*" said Goneril scornfully. "She's not ill, she's *dying*! I poisoned her!"

Regan looked up at Goneril. She parted her lips to speak, but all that came out was a trickle of slime.

"And all for nothing!" Goneril cried. "He's

dead! My beloved Edmund is dead!"

At those words, the light in Regan's eyes went out. Her body stiffened a moment and then was still.

"Don't you dare!" said Goneril. "You think that if you die now, you'll be the first to meet him in the underworld, don't you? Well I will beat you to it, sister!"

Before the doctors could do anything, Goneril had grabbed a dagger and plunged it into her heart.

"We'll see who loves him best," were her last words.

"Before I die," gasped Edmund, "I must see your face, stranger, and know who it is that sends me to hell."

The stranger knelt beside Edmund and removed his mask.

"Edgar, my brother!" Edmund gasped.

"My hands are as bloody as yours; my soul as fit for damnation, I am sure," said Edgar, "but our poor father did not deserve the darkness you plunged him into."

Edmund was going to say something else when Albany's servant returned with the bloody dagger.

"Your wife, my lord," he said, "and her sister – whom she poisoned …"

"Poisoned? What?" Albany seemed bewildered suddenly – as if, after all that had happened, he simply couldn't take in any more.

"… are dead, my lord," the servant said.

Edmund made a strange, gurgling cry. Edgar looked down at his brother to see tears rolling down his cheeks.

"There's someone even you feel sorry for, is that it?" said Edgar.

"There has been too much death," Edmund whispered. "The king and Cordelia—"

"Oh no … no!" said Edgar. "What have you done?"

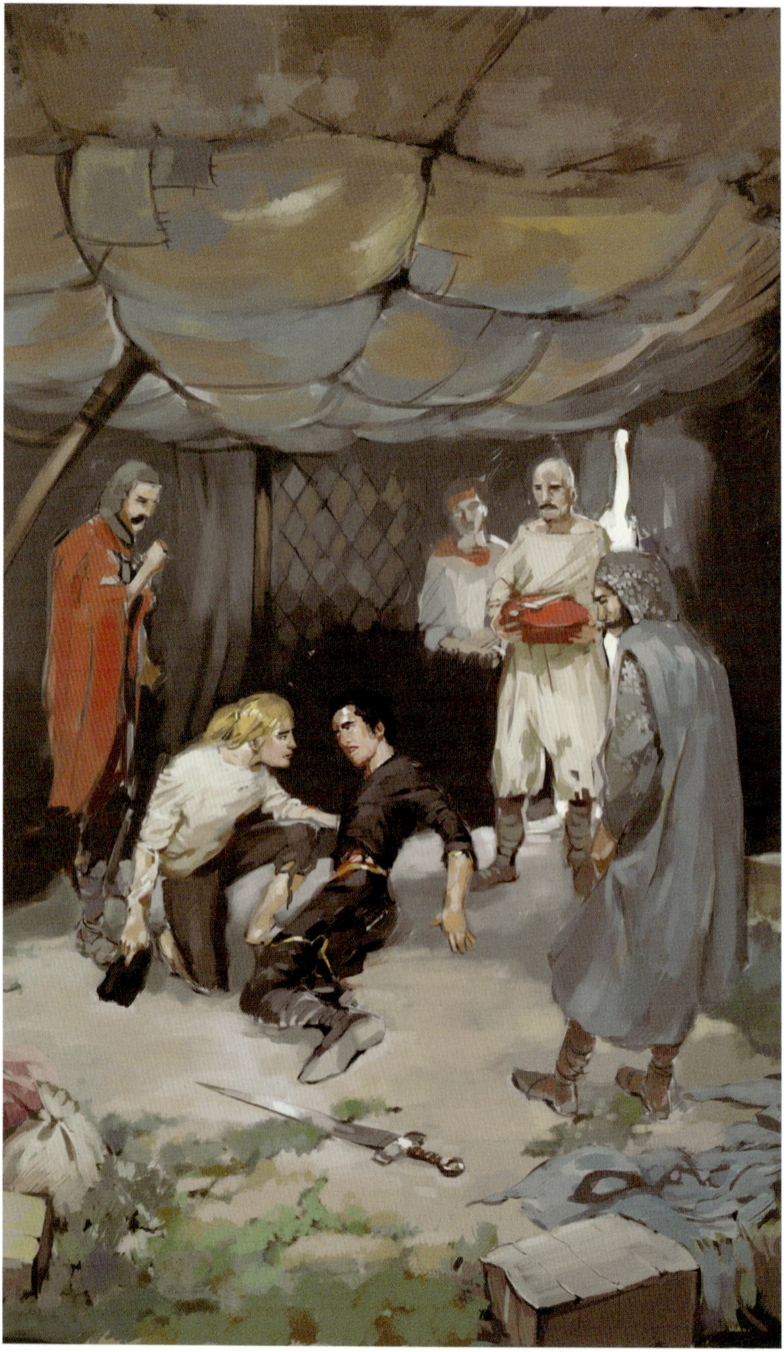

"There may still be time, but you must hurry," Edmund continued. "I sent my captain after them with written orders …"

"What orders?" said Albany.

"That they should be hanged immediately," said Edmund, "so that you Albany, in your foolish mercy, would not have a chance to spare their lives."

"Where are they?" said Edgar, but Edmund gave no answer, though Edgar shook him and shook him. Edmund's head rolled back. He was dead.

"I know the place," said Albany. "It's where we keep all our important prisoners."

"Come on, then!" said Edgar. "Before it's too late."

Edgar and Albany raced through the camp. When they reached the prison, the guards saw the look on Albany's face and hurried to open the gate before he even had time – or breath – to give the order.

"The lord Edmund's captain," Edgar cried. "Has he been here?"

"He's inside now," a guard replied.

"Then perhaps there's still time," said Albany.

He and Edgar pushed past the guards and ran. In moments, they arrived, panting, in the heart of the prison. The door to Lear and Cordelia's cell stood open.

Suddenly, they heard a terrible cry of "No!"

Lear's voice!

"The king is still alive!" said Albany. "Quickly!"

Edgar reached the cell first, but what he saw made him wish he was blind. Lear was struggling with Edmund's captain. Despite his fury, the old man was too weak to stop the captain tying one end of a rope to the bars. From the other end, high above their heads, hung Cordelia's body, twisting silently in the air.

"I have my orders, sirs," the captain began, reaching for the letter Edmund had given him, but − before he had a chance to pull it from his pocket − Lear seized Edgar's sword and ran him through.

Edgar and Albany cut Cordelia down at once. They tried everything they could to get her heart beating again, but it was hopeless: she was dead. At last, they turned to Lear. For a moment he just looked at them, and then he went over and cradled his youngest daughter in his arms.

"Howl," he began to wail. "Howl! Howl! HOWL!" His voice grew louder and louder, until it rang around the cold walls of the prison. "Oh, you are men of stone. How can you see what I have seen and not cry out, so loud that your voices would split the sky? She's dead, don't you understand? Curse you all, I could have saved her! Cordelia, don't go so soon – wait a while. What's that, my love, you want to say something?"

Albany and Edgar looked on sadly as Lear put his ear to Cordelia's dead lips.

"She always had a quiet voice," Lear told them, "a sweet voice. I killed the man who tried to hang you." He spoke as if Cordelia could hear him but when she did not reply, her death pierced his heart afresh.

"Why should a dog, a horse, a *rat* have life – and you no breath at all?" Lear cried. "I shall never see you again. Never, never, never. Wait, what's that? Her lips – look, her lips, they ..."

The sentence was never finished. King Lear, an old and broken man, slumped forward - dead at last.